Charles Meynell

PADRE LIBERATORE and the ONTOLOGISTS

Charles Meynell

PADRE LIBERATORE and the ONTOLOGISTS

ISBN/EAN: 9783741165009

Manufactured in Europe, USA, Canada, Australia, Japa

Cover: Foto ©Andreas Hilbeck / pixelio.de

Manufactured and distributed by brebook publishing software
(www.brebook.com)

Charles Meynell

PADRE LIBERATORE and the ONTOLOGISTS

PADRE LIBERATORE

AND

THE ONTOLOGISTS:

A Review.

BY

THE REV. CHARLES MEYNELL, D.D.

PROFESSOR OF PHILOSOPHY AND LITERATURE AT ST. MARY'S COLLEGE, OSCOTT.

LONDON:

BURNS, OATES, AND CO., 17, 18 PORTMAN STREET,

AND 63 PATERNOSTER ROW.

[The following pages had been intended for insertion in a Catholic periodical. When this design was abandoned, and it was determined to give them a separate publication, the writer found it convenient to retain the form of a review, in which they were originally written. The fact of the recent condemnation, at Rome, of certain philosophical doctrines, will account for the discussion, at the present time, of a work published so long ago as the year 1858.]

PADRE LIBERATORE AND THE ONTOLOGISTS.*

WHAT is Ontologism? It is by no means easy to answer this question satisfactorily. Ontologism, according to F. Liberatore, consists, essentially, in the doctrine that man enjoys in this life a direct and immediate cognition of God; but very few of those who are considered Ontologists really hold the doctrine—at least, in the unqualified sense thus expressed. For instance, the little Ontologistic party in this country did not hold it; while, in America, even Dr. Brownson, jealous as he ever was of any other than himself being the exponent of Ontologistic tenets, quotes with approbation F. Caswall's hymn on the Pure Intuition, in which God is said to be " by nurture, meditation, grace, *reflexively revealed.*" Hence it is that, although the doctrine of a direct, immediate knowledge of God has been pronounced by the authorities at Rome as unsafe to be taught, yet the Ontologists will not allow that they have been condemned. Besides, F. Liberatore refutes " moderate Ontologists," " semi-Ontologists," and all sorts of persons Ontologistically inclined—amongst the rest, Rosmini-Serbati;† and this very fact shows that we have not yet got to the root of the matter; for if Ontologism consisted

---

* *Della Conoscenza Intellettuale.* Trattato di MATTEO LIBERATORE, D.C.D.G. Roma: Uffizio della *Civiltà Cattolica.* 1858.

† F. Liberatore declares in one place that Rosmini was " certainly not an Ontologist;" but it will be seen that our author uses the term sometimes in a strict, and sometimes in a wider, sense, according to the distinction laid down in the present article. There can be no doubt that Rosmini was, as he is generally reputed to have been, an Ontologist in the broader sense of the word.

merely in the aforesaid doctrine, a semi-Ontologist would be impossible: either he would hold the doctrine, or not; and if he did not hold it, he would not be even a semi-Ontologist. Perhaps Ontologism consists in holding the doctrine of *innate ideas*—or, at least, in maintaining that there is something *à priori* in thought, beyond the mere native force of the mind itself; but, according to F. Liberatore, Ontologism does not date earlier than Cartesianism; while the doctrine of an *à-priori* element in thought, taught in one shape or another, is, surely, as old as philosophy itself. Does Ontologism consist, as somebody has suggested, in the recognition of the objective character of Necessary Truth? But what Catholic would deny that Necessary Truth is objective? Why, according to this account, we are all Ontologists! This is always the way: there will be no end of fruitless disputation, until people will settle definitely what they can agree amongst themselves to differ about.

We cannot compel others to use words in the same sense in which we use them ourselves; but, at any rate, we can discover in what sense they and we respectively use them. Ontologism means, in one signification of the word, not any one philosophical system, but a line of thought which pervades many, in other respects, very different systems. This is the sense in which Ontologists use the word when they tell us that they have not been condemned at Rome: and this is also the sense in which F. Liberatore uses the word when he speaks of moderate Ontologists and semi-Ontologists, and when he calls Descartes an Ontologist—they have the virus of error, the principle of the evil; and, if they carried out this principle consistently, if only they embodied their views in an adequate system, they would be condemned by all orthodox thinkers. But, besides this, there is the narrow sense of the word Ontologism, the fundamental doctrine of which is the intellectual vision of God; and in this sense no one can deny that the S. Congregation has condemned Ontologism.

The next question to be asked is, What is that broader sense of the word in which there are degrees of Ontologism? F. Liberatore has, we believe, in no one single passage determined this; but there can be little doubt, from what he says in one place and another, that whoever admits an *à-priori*, positive, objective element in thought, distinct from the mind itself, and stamped with the characters of necessity and universality, is virtually an Ontologist. It would be superfluous to burden these pages with proofs of a statement which no reader of the *Conoscenza Intellettuale* will call in question. Hence it is that even Descartes is called by F. Liberatore an Ontologist; and Kant, also, on account of his *à-priori* element, and synthetical judgments *à priori*, is an Ontologist; indeed, the philosophy of Kant is made to account for that of Gioberti —and, in a sense, with some show of reason. Hence, too, the swarm of living Ontologists with whom the writer is at war. They read the modern books, and have bemuddled their brains with the mists of transcendentalism; they have neglected St. Thomas; they cannot read him, or they read him only to pervert his meaning, by attaching a modern sense to his words and phrases, quite alien to their real sense. And Descartes is to blame for all this: he ruined philosophical studies by revolutionising the method, and the science has been a failure ever since. Well, we shall not enter into this portion of the subject further than to remark, that here the writer and his opponents are at one. The Ontologists equally deplore the revolution effected by Descartes, and possess as ardent a desire for the revival of scholastic studies.

The refutation, then, of Ontologism in all its various shapes and phases, and the substitution for it of a system based on the venerated teaching of St. Thomas Aquinas, is the object of the *Conoscenza Intellettuale*. We shall not be concerned in these pages to decide on the controversy which has chiefly called it forth, but merely to sketch out the main features of the author's teaching, and consider their bearings on a question which thinkers of every school must agree in regarding as one of the gravest speculative questions of the day. As to the writer of the work himself, Ontologists must certainly regard him as a very formidable antagonist—both from the position he holds as an exponent of orthodox views in philosophy, with such high sanction, and from his exquisitely subtle

6

power of analysis, the natural strength of which has been fostered by communion with the Master Mind. Nor ought they to regard this as a misfortune. Philosophical, like religious truth, ever grows and waxes strong by opposition; and if, after all, they are right, the issue will be surely in their favour; and if, on the other hand, they are wrong, Ontologism may linger for a time, but it will be gradually and tacitly relinquished—first, by the ablest minds of the school, and at last by the mass. As matters stand, it seems (but we speak under correction) that there is no recent system of Ontologism which the authorities will sanction as safe to be taught, excepting that of Rosmini: and some may, perhaps, deny that Rosmini is an Ontologist; while others will consider that his system, as it stands, is untenable. However this be, we rejoice to see that F. Liberatore, while refuting this author's system, acknowledges, in the most gracious manner, his remarkable talents as a speculative thinker. It is no slight praise, for instance, to attribute to him so large a share in the victory over that miserable sensationalism which, not so very long ago, reigned throughout the continental schools.

In the criticism upon which we are now about to enter, we may fairly distinguish between the writer and the philosopher—between the controversial skirmisher in the *Civiltà Cattolica*, and the commentator on St. Thomas. And, indeed, such a distinction is necessary to be made, if we would do F. Liberatore justice. For it must be admitted, even by his warmest admirers, that he has grave faults; and we intend to speak of them most frankly. In the former portion of the work, for instance, where he is chiefly considering the authorities on whom his opponents rely for the support of their Ontologistic tenets, he argues like a man in a suppressed rage: he rebukes, taunts, and even reviles; he argues at them *de haut en bas;* he preaches, he scolds, he ridicules; he connects their doctrines with pantheistic realists of the past, and with pantheists of recent times; with Averröes and Scotus Erigena; with Amaury de Chartres and David de Dinant;* with

* Both Amaury and David were pantheists. The key-note of their

7

Spinoza, with Schelling, and with Hegel. These be your gods, O Israel! There are your Ontologists, if any were before Descartes, there your Ontologists after! Now, we all know very well what is meant by this sort of language, and what it is worth. It is just the same when a fiery Thomist divine calls a disciple of Suarez a Pelagian, or the disciple of Suarez calls the Thomist a Calvinist. It is mere *odium philosophicum;* but it is worse; it is what a certain writer calls "poisoning the wells." They do not all know its worth who read the *Civiltà Cattolica;* and what is there said with a very intelligible mental reservation, these will receive as said in downright earnest. All this is *ad captandum.* And it is *ad captandum* to quote the trite text from Rom. i., which declares that we know the Creator from "the visible things of His creation"—because Ontologism, as such, does not deny the *à-posteriori* proofs for the existence of God; it is *ad captandum,* also, to speak of the doctrine of a mere mental intuition of God as transferring to earth that vision which is the privilege of the blessed in heaven,* and to cite against his opponents the text, "No man hath seen God at any time"—because no Ontologist ever supposed that, in the mental intuition, God is seen *sicuti est;* and the text of Scripture, taken too rigorously, would also exclude that spiritual vision of the Face of God, so often insisted upon in Holy Scripture as the privilege of the just and clean of heart. And whether the Ontologists can claim St. Augustine, St. Anselm, and St. Buonaventure, or no, it is simply unjust and untrue to say so broadly as F.

system was, "Omnia esse Unum, et omnia esse Deum." But, between the doctrine of the former and that of the latter, St. Thomas marks this difference, that with Amaury God was the formal, while with David He was the material, principle of things—in fact, the *Prima Materia* itself. To connect one's opponents, no sufficient cause being assigned, with writers of this class, or pantheistic commentators of Aristotle—like Averröes—by way of *argumentum ad pietatem,* is not merely unfair, *it is cruel.*

* "Era ben naturale che in un tempo, in cui il progresso ci fa sapere che la beatitudine dee procacciarsi sulla terra, venisse quaggiu trasferita quella visione, che veramente è propria della felicità sempiterna: *non ridebit me homo et vivet*" (vol. i. art. i. p. 68).

Liberatore says it, that there is absolutely no sort of countenance for Ontologistic tenets in the writings of these Fathers. Let us revive the study of St. Thomas, by all means; and, if possible, let us also revive the serene philosophical temper of our master. The writer's faults are, however, to be excused, in great measure, by the circumstances of his position. The controversial attitude is itself unfavourable to speculation; and the office of exponent of orthodox views in philosophy, a nice and delicate one. No wonder if he sometimes speaks rather from the professorial chair, than as one speaking amongst equals; and, if he sometimes scolds, the occasional downright scurrility of Gioberti was enough to provoke a saint.* Allowances ought also to be made on the score of the Italian temperament, in which *odium philosophicum*, or *theologicum*, becomes sometimes a kind of rabies. But for garbling and misquoting authorities there is no excuse; and F. Liberatore sins on both these heads, as will appear in the sequel.

The wise men came from the East; and so, according to Gioberti, did the Ontologists. Their transcendental doctrine passed over into Greece, where it was taught by Pythagoras; and from him was transferred, through Socrates, into Plato. From Plato it was borrowed by the Fathers of the Church; who, in their turn, communicated it to the schoolmen. The tradition was somewhat disturbed by nominalists and conceptualists; but it was perpetuated by the realists, until the miserable psychologism of Descartes almost succeeded in effac-.ing it, when it was happily restored, but imperfectly, by Rosmini; and perfectly, of course, by Gioberti himself. The Ontologists depend, for the authority and orthodoxy of their teaching, upon such eminent names as those of St. Augustine, St. Anselm, and St. Buonaventure; and they have even ventured to quote in their favour a very remarkable article in the

* For instance, in speaking of the connection of the Idea with the Word as "the Ontological basis of the moral and absolute precept of veracity," he has the following words on the casuists: "La Chiesa Cattolica (*se si eccettua qualche oscuro ed impuro casista*), . . . non ammise mai la distinzione del falsiloquio dalla bugia," &c. (note 3 in tom. ii.)

Summa of St. Thomas. We shall, following F. Liberatore, consider these authorities—not in the chronological order, but in that of their supposed weight in countenancing Ontologism. To begin, then, with St. Buonaventure.

The *Itinerarium* of St. Buonaventure contains some of the most formidable statements that the Ontologists can adduce, as authorising the main features of their teaching. But as all who are interested in the present controversy will by this time have got them almost by heart, we will aim at being as succinct as possible in our exposition of them.

The renowned author of this beautiful tract declares that God is " the Reason of all things, and the infallible Rule and Light of Truth, in which all things shine forth." He endorses the sentiment of St. Augustine, that " the light of every one who truly reasons is lighted up by this Truth;" so that our intellect " is conjoined to the Eternal Truth itself, since, except by the teaching of such Truth, it apprehends nothing as certitudinally true." He says that in three modes the mind can contemplate God: as He is without us, within us, and above us—*extra nos, intra nos, et supra nos.* We contemplate Him without us by His footprints in creation (*per vestigium*); within us by His image, which is within our soul (*per imaginem*); and above us by His Light, which is sealed upon our mind (*per Lumen*)—in allusion to the text, " Signatum est super nos Lumen vultus Tui, Domine."* The consideration of God as contemplated " above us" is treated of in the fifth chapter of the *Itinerarium*, which commences with explaining that " the Light which is sealed upon us is the Light of Eternal Truth, since our mind is immediately informed by the Truth itself;" and it is in this portion of the work that we are introduced to the vision of God under the idea of Pure Being which has been so often quoted, and which therefore we shall abstain from quoting again.

Here, then, the question occurs to be asked, whether this teaching of St. Buonaventure be identical with the Ontologism which has been recently condemned at Rome? We shall see presently. Meantime, F. Liberatore has many things to say

* Psalm iv.

upon the subject; and we regret to state that almost every
thing he says is either untrue or irrelevant. In the first place,
he cites a passage from the Saint's Commentary on the " Sentences," which, certainly, as distinctly contradicts the fundamental doctrine of Ontologism as any language can : " *Cum
nos non cognoscamus Deum, nisi per creaturas ; nos Eum non
nominamus nisi per nomina creaturarum.*" But where did F.
Liberatore get this quotation from? Did he read it himself in
the Commentary, or pick it up at second hand? Has he no
friends or no enemies? Was there nobody to point out to
him, long before now, that he is making here a very extra-
ordinary blunder ; and that, although the words quoted occur
in the place referred to, yet they occur only to be set aside,
as expressing a doctrine which the author of the Commentary
distinctly rejects? " Sed hæc positio," he says, " non videtur
stare." (!)*   Only fancy St. Buonaventure (or F. Liberatore

---

* St. Buonaventure propounds the question, "An omnia divina
nomina translatitia sunt?" (in lib. i. Dist. xxii. Quæst. 3). He lays down
the arguments *pro* and *contra.* One of the arguments in favour of the
affirmative statement is, " Unum quodque sicut contingit intelligere,
contingit et significare : sed non contingit Deum intelligi nisi per pro-
prietates et conditiones creaturarum : ergo nec nominare." It is, however, counter-argued that " *Quædam dicuntur de Deo quæ habent oppositum
in omni creaturd ; ut æternitas et immensitas.*" The conclusion is negative : "Non omnia quæ de Deo dicuntur translativa censeri debent, cum
quædam proprie dicantur, licet nonnulla secundum similitudinem de Ipso
verificentur." Then follow the *Responsiones ad Argumenta,* containing
the words abused by F. Liberatore :
" *Resp. ad Arg.* AD HOC QUIDAM VOLUERUNT DICERE quod quædam
sunt nomina quæ Deus Sibi imposuit : quædam quæ nos Ei imposuimus.
Si loquamur de nominibus quæ Deus Sibi imposuit, cum Ipse se proprie
intelligat, hujusmodi nomina sunt propria, et talia dicuntur esse BONUM
et QUI EST. Unde Dionysius videtur velle quòd illud nomen, *Bonum,*
solum sit proprium et principale ; Damascenus quòd illud nomen, *Qui Est,*
sit solum et principale ; et unus attendit in nomine perfectionem, alter abso-
lutionem ; uterque tamen proprietatem. Si autem loquamur de nominibus
quæ nos Ei imposuimus, sic *cum nos non cognoscamus Deum nisi per
creaturas, nos Eum non nominamus nisi per nomina creaturarum ;* ideo
solum translativè, sive quia propriùs et prius conveniunt creaturæ, sive
quia prius imposita sunt creaturæ, quamvis non propriùs conveniant

himself, for that matter, since he tacitly endorses the opinion) teaching that we only name God by the names which we give to creatures. F. Liberatore also says that this is an ascetical work, "quite full of mystical senses and figures of speech," and therefore one must not seek in it "logical severity and precision of scientific words;" that its purpose is "not so much to instruct the intellect as to inflame the will;" that the last chapter speaks of "ecstasies and rapts in God"—matters about which we must inquire of Grace, and not of doctrine— quoting, "Si quæris quomodo hæc fiant, interroga Gratiam non doctrinam;" and he advises his opponents to read the profound scientific works of St. Buonaventure, and especially the Commentary. Now, we feel bound to state, merely in the interests of literary justice, that, although the *Itinerarium* does certainly contain "figures of speech and mystical senses," yet that the author gives to them a most unmistakably meta-

creaturæ. Et hæc est translatio quædam, quamvis propriè loquendo sit translatio, quando propriùs conveniunt iis a quibus transferuntur; ut ridere hominibus propriùs quam pratis. SED HÆC POSITIO NON VIDETUR STARE. Cum enim nos cognoscamus Deum tripliciter, scilicet, per effectum, per excellentiam, et per ablationem, constat quòd omnibus his modis contingit Deum nominare. Si per effectum, nulla est ibi translatio. Pariformiter si per excellentiam. Similiter si per ablationem," &c.

The reader will see that it is utterly impossible F. Liberatore (or the author from whom he copied the passage quoted, supposing he copied it) could have read the article in which it occurs. He simply glanced over the matter to pick out a text wherewith to combat the Ontologists, and has made a most unhappy selection. The quotation is accompanied, as we have said, by an admonition, addressed to his opponents, to read the profound doctrinal writings of St. Buonaventure on the *Sentences;* and also by an intimation that there are very many other passages to the same purpose, *i. e.* that we only name God by the names we give to creatures! "Se si vuol conoscere qual sia l'opinione di S. Buonaventura nella presente quistione, si leggano le altre sue opere dottrinali, e segnamente i profondi suoi scritti sopra il Maestro delle sentenze. In essi sono moltissimi luoghi (!) ne' quali il S. Dottore dichiara espressamente di non amettere altra cognizione di Dio nei termini naturali, se non quella che si astrae dalla considerazione delle cose create. Basterà per tutti *questo sol passo, di cui niente può esserci di più esplicito :* Cum nos non cognoscamus," &c.

physical interpretation: the six wings of the Seraphim, for
instance, which Isaias saw in vision, are six natural powers,
viz. "sensus, imaginatio, ratio, intellectus, intelligentia, syn-
deresis;" that, so far from the work being wanting in logical
precision and scientific terms, it is simply unintelligible, except
to the philosophically educated; that the pages are absolutely
crowded with scientific terms, and the writer instructs the
intellect through them in a most definite matter, though, of
course, his purpose is religious and ascetical; and that, as to
the state of ecstasy, to which alone the admonition " Interroga
Gratiam" refers, it is not treated of until the last chapter, and
has nothing to do with the author's metaphysics. There, following St. Dionysius the Areopagite,* he leaves behind, he
transcends, metaphysics, though still expressing himself in
scientific language : " Sensus desere" (he says), " et intellect-
uales operationes, et sensibilia, et invisibilia, et *omne non ens et
ens,* et ad unitatem (ut possibile est) inscius restituere Ipsius,
Qui est super omnem essentiam et scientiam." This is the
supernatural contemplation of God in ecstasy, and something
very different from the natural contemplation of Him under
the conception of Ens, described in ch. v. But since F.
Liberatore refers his opponents to the Commentary for the real
opinion of St. Buonaventure, to the Commentary we will go
with them. Yet there we find the same teaching as in the
Itinerarium ! There are the same three modes of knowing
God—*per vestigium, per imaginem,* and *per Lumen;* and
still the same lofty language reiterated in divers places as to
the last mode : " Tertius gradus est ab animâ in Deum, *quia
imago ab Ipsâ Veritate formatur, et Deo immediatè conjungitur*"
(in lib. i. Sent. Dist. iii. Qu. 2).

And now we are delighted to pass on to the one point, on
this portion of the subject, as to which we can fully agree
with F. Liberatore ; and it is a very important one. St.
Buonaventure (in lib. *Sent.* ii. Dist. xxxiv. Qu. 4) distinctly
denies the doctrine of innate ideas : Ideas, he says, are
" acquired *by means of sense and experience.*† Now, it is im-

* *De Mysticâ Theologiâ*, cap. i.
† Alluding to a passage of Boetius, he says : " Quod voluerunt aliqui

possible not to interpret the passage of the *Itinerarium*, in which he speaks of the mental vision of God, under the conception of Being, in the light of this clear statement. Wishing to contemplate God, not by His footprints, or His image, but in Himself, he took a conception to represent Him, which is at once the loftiest and the weakest of our intellect. This conception is, as he tells us, the first that occurs to the mind, and one which enters as an essential element into every other conception; but, then, it is not innate, but an abstraction made by the Active Intellect (*intellectus agens*). On this head St. Buonaventure is strictly at one with St. Thomas. But, of course, the vision of God as Pure Being breaks down, for the very obvious psychological reason that it wants *marks;* it has not what the logicians call *intension* or *comprehension;* that is to say, Being, in general, is nothing in particular; and this result is expressed by the Saint when he says, " *videtur sibi nihil videre!*" It is naturally distasteful to us to have to compare Gioberti with St. Buonaventure; but we must remark that, when the former expresses himself in somewhat the same fashion about his own mental vision of God, which fails for the reason assigned, F. Liberatore speaks of it with contempt. He calls it a " muddle" (*imbroglio*), and says that Gioberti himself does not know whether it deserve the name of knowledge or not. Are we to have two weights and two measures in philosophy, or is F. Liberatore prepared to treat St. Buonaventure's vision as he treats that of Gioberti? However, there is this wide difference between the former vision and that of Gioberti and the Ontologists: the Being of the one is acquired by experience, and is an offspring of the mind's abstractive power; while that of the latter is *à priori*, and is

intelligi sic : quòd intellectus noster dicatur habere apud se cognitionem universalium habitualem innatam; alioquin non posset per virtutem suam, abstrahendo etiam a sensibus, et a phantasmatibus facere intellectum possibile actu intelligentem : omne enim quod deducit alterum de potentiâ ad actum, est ens in actu. Sed iste modus dicendi verbis Philosophi non consonat, qui dicit, animam esse creatam sicut tabulam rasam; nec habere cognitionem habituum sibi innatam, sed acquirere mediante sensu et experientiâ.

God Himself. St. Buonaventure, therefore, is not an Ontologist, in the narrow sense of the word, and according to the
distinction laid down by us in the beginning. But is he not
an Ontologist in the wider sense of the word?—because,
although he does not hold that the Idea is innate, yet does he
not hold that it has its source in the Intellectual Light, which
he does not scruple to identify with God Himself? Now, F.
Liberatore assures us that the teaching of St. Buonaventure,
as to the whole question of Ontologism, is strictly in accord-
ance with that of St. Thomas; so we will defer the answer to
this question until we come to consider the opinions of the
latter.

In speaking of the remaining authorities, excepting, of
course, St. Thomas, we shall be more brief, since, as F.
Liberatore truly says, the matter in their case is clearer. He
quotes St. Anselm as affirming "that the human mind, in
seeing the Intellectual Light, sees God." The Saint asks,
"Aut potuit [anima] aliquid intelligere de Te, nisi per
Lumen Tuam et Veritatem? Si ergo vidit lucem et
veritatem, vidit Te" (*Prosologium* xiv.).* F. Liberatore

* As nothing can be more unsatisfactory than scraps from authorities,
we beg to submit to the reader as much of the context as is necessary to
show the writer's drift: "An invenisti, anima mea, quod quærebas?
Quærebas Deum, invenisti Eum esse quiddam summum omnium, quo
nihil melius cogitari potest; et hoc esse vitam ipsam, lucem, sapientiam,
bonitatem, æternam beatitudinem, et beatam æternitatem; et hoc esse
ubique et semper. . . . . Cur non Te sentit, Domine Deus, anima mea,
si invenit Te? An non invenit Quem invenit esse Lucem et Veritatem?
Quomodo namque intellexit hoc, nisi videndo Lucem et Veritatem?
Si ergo vidit Lucem et Veritatem, vidit Te: si non vidit Te, non vidit
Lucem nec Veritatem. An et Veritas et Lux est quod vidit; et tamen
nondum Te vidit; quia vidit Te aliquatenus, sed non vidit Te sicuti es.
Domine Deus meus, formator et reformator meus, dic desideranti
animæ meæ quid aliud es quam quod vidit, ut pure videat quod desiderat.
Intendit se ut plus videat, et nihil videt ultra hoc quod vidit, nisi tenebras. Immo non videt tenebras, quæ nullæ sunt in Te; sed videt se non
plus videre, propter tenebras suas. Cur hoc, Domine, cur hoc? Tenebratur oculus ejus infirmitate suâ, aut reverberatur fulgore Tuo?
Sed certè et tenebratur in se et reverberatur a Te. Utique et obscuratur
suâ brevitate, et obruitur Tuâ Immensitate. Verè et contrahitur angustiâ

acknowledges that this passage seems, at the first blush, to countenance Ontologism; but he considers that it is one thing to see God's Light, and another to see God Himself: now, it is of the essence of Ontologism to say that we see God Himself. Very well; but could not a similar excuse be framed for Malebranche, who, although he taught that the mind has a direct, immediate vision of God, yet seems to explain away the doctrine in the statement of it? "Minds do not see the Divine Substance, taken absolutely," he says, "but only inasmuch as related to creatures, or participable by them."* However this be, it is clear enough that St. Anselm is Ontologist, in the broader sense of the word, according to the distinction we have laid down. Then why not admit as much at once, and make an end of it, instead of quoting such passages as, "Nunquam Te vidi, Domine Deus meus," which the mass, at any rate, of those who call themselves Ontologists would heartily endorse? Besides, St. Anselm (and, by the by, St. Buonaventure also) admits the *à-priori* proof of God's existence, drawn from the idea of a sovereignly perfect Being. Well, on the authority of St. Thomas, F. Liberatore ventures to differ from these writers. He says that reasoning in this manner is "making an arbitrary transit from the ideal to the real order." But is it possible that their subtle minds should not have been aware of this very obvious objection? Nothing, indeed, could warrant such a mode of reasoning as theirs, excepting the consideration that they held an *à-priori*, objective element in thought, as the account of the idea of a Most Perfect Being. We shall not enter here into the question whether this kind of argument for the existence of God can stand criticism or no: there are other *à-priori* proofs beside this one. But all *à-priori* proofs must necessarily suppose an *à-priori*, objective element

suâ, et vincitur amplitudine Tuâ. Quanta namque est Lux illa de quâ micat omne verum quo rationali menti lucet? Quam ampla est illa Veritas, in quâ est omne quod verum est, et extra quam non nisi nihil et falsum est! Quam immensa est quæ uno intuito videt quæcunque facta, et a quo, et per Quem, et quomodo de nihilo facta sunt! Quid puritatis, quid simplicitatis, quid certitudinis et splendoris ibi est! Certè plus plus-quam a creaturâ valeat intelligi" (*Prosol. ad loc. citat.*)

* *Recherche de la Vérité*, livre iii. ; *De l'Esprit pur*, part ii. ch. vi.

in thought. F. Liberatore seems quite aware of this; however, he says that it "has nothing to do with Ontologism," which consists in doctrines of an immediate knowledge or vision of a God. Be it so; but, then, we cannot play fast and loose, in this manner, with the word Ontologism. Let us hear no more of moderate Ontologists or semi-Ontologists, unless St. Anselm and St. Buonaventure are reckoned amongst the number.

Passing on now to St. Augustine. Just as F. Liberatore had commenced his infelicitous comments on the *Itinerarium* by recommending to his opponents the perusal of the profound scientific works of St. Buonaventure, so now, in speaking of St. Augustine, he recommends to them "the examination of those passages in which he sets himself *ex-professo* to treat" of "the manner in which we see God in this life." Such passages, he thinks, are chiefly to be found in the chapter, *De Ideis*, of the book, *De Diversis Quæstionibus*, lxxxiii.; and in the letter, *De Deo Videndo*, addressed to Paulina. But the short chapter, *De Ideis*, considers the Ideas, chiefly, as they are in the Divine Mind, and (according to the interpretation of St. Thomas)* as contemplated by the purified soul in the Beatific Vision; while the letter to Paulina, also, is rather a treatise *ex-professo* on the manner of seeing God in the next life,—or, if at all in this, the vision is *oculis cordis nostri*, proper to the just and clean of heart, and has nothing to do with metaphysics. "Qui didicerunt a Domino Jesu Christo mites esse et humiles corde," he says, "plus cogitando et orando proficiunt [in hâc inquisitione], quam legendo et audiendo."† Is it worth while (especially as we agree with F. Liberatore, that St. Augustine taught none of the somewhat silly-looking propositions recently condemned by the S. Congregation as

---

* "Quod autem Augustinus non sic intellexerit omnia cognosci in rationibus æternis, vel in Incommutabili Veritate, quasi ipsæ rationes æternæ videantur, patet per hoc, quod ipse dicit in libro lxxxiii. (*Quæst.* Qu. 46, a med. tom. 4), quod *rationalis anima non omnis et quæcunque, sed quæ sancta et pura fuerit, asseritur illi visioni esse, scilicet rationum æternarum esse idonea; sicut sunt animæ beatorum*" (Pr. Sec. Qu. lxxxiv. ō).

† *Ep. ad Paulinam*, 1.

Ontologism) to examine the passages which our author has strung together, chiefly from these sources, for the purpose of showing that the Holy Doctor was not, strictly speaking, an Ontologist?—because, in one place, " he affirms that the soul only contemplates *the Ideas* by means of the intellect, which is, as it were, its spiritual and inward eye;" in another, " that this is not the privilege of every soul, but only of that which shall be holy and pure;" in another, that we do not see God " sicut nos videmus hunc solem, vel mentis obtutu;" in another (which also Malebranche said), " that we do not see the substance of God;" in another, " that we do not see the Creative Force;" in another, that the vision belongs to "the clean of heart." All, or nearly all of this, is either irrelevant, or merely *ad captandum*. But F. Liberatore says the Ontologists do maintain that we see the " Creative Force;" and it is true that Gioberti said something of the kind, which we find repeated after him by Branchereau; but, then, they both explain it away by a truism. For the rest, it has nothing to do with the question. Whatever St. Augustine is speaking about in these passages, he speaks in others of a very definite doctrine, which St. Thomas and St. Augustine himself expressly tell us that he derived from Plato. The knowledge of God, then, is that which Plato had of Him—not that which is proper to holy souls, but which is common to all men. But since at the end of this portion of the controversy F. Liberatore introduces St. Thomas as the interpreter of St. Augustine, we shall here proceed also to consider the teaching of this " angel of the schools," and, at the same time, we shall consider F. Liberatore in the far more favourable character of interpreter of St. Thomas.

The opinion of St. Thomas regarding the nature of the Intellectual Light is to be found in the fifth article of the eighty-fourth Question, *prim. sec.*, in which it is asked, whether the human mind knows immaterial things in their eternal reasons? The conclusion is affirmative, because " Augustinus dicit" (*Confess.* lib. xii.), " Si ambo videmus verum esse quod dicis, et ambo videmus verum esse quod dico, ubi quæso id videmus? Nec ego utique in te, nec tu in me, sed

B

ambo in ipsâ, quæ est supra mentes nostras, incommutabile veritate." But it is objected that, if we see the " eternal reasons," we must see God Himself, in whom the eternal reasons subsist; that Scripture tells us that the invisible things of God are " understood by the things that are made;" and that this is sheer Platonism. So that we have the Angelic Doctor here in the interesting position of answering the objections of those who would accuse him of being what is now called an Ontologist. And how does he reply? Why, he simply admits that he *platonises* here : " Qui philosophi vocantur si quâ forte vera, et fidei nostræ accommoda dixerunt, ab eis, tamquam ab injustis possessoribus, in usum nostrum vindicanda sunt." He accepted Plato's doctrine then, he tells us; but he qualified it, and he qualified it as St. Augustine qualified it. For Plato gave to the Ideas a separate subsistence,* but St. Augustine " laid down that the ' reasons' of all creatures, according to which all things are fashioned, and according to which also the human soul knows all things, existed in the Divine Mind." St. Thomas also introduced another qualification. According to the Platonicians, the sole participation of the " eternal reasons" sufficed for knowledge ; but he postulated, " besides the Intellectual Light, intelligible species received from things, for the knowledge of material things."

But if it be objected, " How can we know the ' eternal reasons,' since these are in the Mind of God, and this would imply that we know God?" St. Thomas answers, that St. Augustine is not to be thus misunderstood,—that the vision of *the eternal reasons themselves* is not the privilege of every soul,

---

* It is at least very doubtful whether Plato himself gave to the Ideas a separate subsistence. From certain passages in the sixth and seventh chapters of the *Republic*, V. Cousin infers that Plato placed the Ideas in the mind of God, as did St. Augustine. For instance, in the sixth book of the *Republic*, we read : " We may say, therefore, as to things cognisable by the intellect, that they become cognisable, not only from The Good [God], by which they are known, but likewise that their being and essence are thence derived ; whilst the Good itself is not essence, but beyond essence, and superior to both in dignity and power" (ch. xix.). *See also Note at the foot of the following page.*

but only of the one "that shall be pure and good." But there
is another mode in which the eternal reasons can be known,
and that is in " the Principle of cognition ;" " sicut si dicamus
quod in solo videntur ea quæ videntur per solom; et sic
necesse est dicere quod anima humana omnia cognoscit in
rationibus æternis per quarum participationem omnia cognos-
cimus." He means (we suppose) that just as the light of
the sun contains virtually all the various colours which are
refracted by the objects which it enlightens, so also does the
Light of Intellect contain virtually, or potentially, those
various truths, which, however, are only reduced to act by
knowledge of actual objects. It is of this Light of the Intellect, he tells us, that the Psalmist speaks, where he says, "The
Light of Thy Countenance, O Lord, is signed upon us"—the
stock text of the Ontologists. The comparison of the light of
the sun with the light of intellect, if it be not sufficiently obvious, might have been suggested by a passage which occurs
in the seventh book of Plato's *Republic*, in which God is
represented as King of the intellectual order, as the sun is king
of the visible order of creation *—at least, St. Thomas shows us
that he was aware of the passage, through Themistius. So far,
it appears that St. Augustine, according to St. Thomas, and
St. Thomas himself, were of the school of moderate realists.
And how does a moderate realist differ from a moderate
Ontologist?

There is, however, a very important passage of the *article*
in question, which appears to favour a somewhat different
conclusion—as far, at least, as St. Thomas is concerned ; and
we intend to give F. Liberatore the fullest advantage of it. St.
Augustine had qualified the doctrine of Plato in the manner

* " As respects appearances, then, it thus seems, that, in the subjects of
human knowledge, the idea of the Good is the last object of vision, and
hard to be seen ; and when beheld, it must be inferred from reason to be
the cause of what is right and beautiful in all things, generating in it
what is visible, both light and its parent [the sun] also ; while in that
which is intelligible, it is itself the Sovereign, producing truth and intelligence; and it must be seen, too, by him that would act with judgment,
either privately or in public."—*The Republic*, vii. 3.

described above, but St. Thomas in nothing qualified the doctrine of St. Augustine. He simply endorses it; and in endorsing it, he tacitly endorses the strong language of the latter as to the Intellectual Light. Now, no language can be more explicit than that in which St. Augustine identifies this Light with God Himself. "Insinuavit nobis [Christus]," he says, "animam humanam et mentem rationalem, quæ inest homini, non inest pecori, non vegetari, non beatificari, non illuminari, nisi ab IPSÂ SUBSTANTIÂ DEI." * And yet, when St. Thomas himself speaks upon the subject, he uses the most qualified and guarded language. "The Intellectual Light," he says, "is a certain participated likeness (*participata similitudo*) of the Uncreated Light in which are seen the eternal reasons." This is certainly very different language from that of St. Augustine. What are we to think? Is the Light, in which we see the eternal reasons, God Himself, or is it only a resemblance of God? The passage, as it stands, is ambiguous. It is open, on the one hand, to say with a certain "subtle Ontologist" whom F. Liberatore quotes, that the Light is said to be *like God*, not because it is not God, but because, in us, it is limited and restricted by the finite conditions of the creature; or to say, on the other hand, with F. Liberatore himself, that it is a mere likeness of the Divine Light. (We ought to remark here, by the way, that the word "imitation" does not exactly render the expression, *participata similitudo;* whereas F. Liberatore, by using indifferently "participated likeness" and "imitation," seems to regard them as equivalents.) Now, is it not possible that St. Thomas *tacitly* qualified the doctrine of St. Augustine on this point, wishing, in the manner of expression, to leave it an open question whether or not the Light were God Himself, and merely stating what, on all hands, it must, at the least, be considered to be? The form of expression,

---

* It will be said, perhaps, that it appears from the context of this passage (*In Joann. Evang. Tract.* xxiii. 5) that St. Augustine speaks here of the supernatural, and not of the natural order; but, to exclude all possibility of cavilling, we contend that it is clear from the context (as, indeed, from the passage itself) that he is speaking of both; else the " vegetari," which has clearly nothing to do with Grace, had not been mentioned.

"*quædam* participata similitudo," seems to favour this view. And it must be remembered that the spirit of St. Thomas was preëminently a spirit of moderation, and he wrote amidst the contentions of realists and nominalists—the former of whom identified the eternal reasons with God Himself, while the latter reduced them either to general names, or, at most, to mere general notions. His conclusions, for the most part, trim neatly between extreme statements. F. Liberatore calls him a realist; but he admitted the fundamental doctrine of the conceptualists, that nothing exists, objectively, besides the individuals with that ratio of resemblance which is the foundation of the "universals." If he be realist at all, it is only in his teaching about the Intellectual Light, wherein even Hauréau considers him to be realist; but it is just here that F. Liberatore considers that he is not realist. The other passages quoted in favour of the "imitation" theory make no stronger case for it than the one in question, if they do not really make against it. Any how, the difficulty still remains, that St. Thomas endorsed the opinion of St. Augustine, while the latter said, and reiterated with all the force of which human language is capable, that the Light is God Himself; while the same unmistakable language was reëchoed by St. Anselm and St. Buonaventure. What says our author to this? Why, it is simply no difficulty to him at all. He is so secure upon this point, that he can afford to laugh at his opponents. But he shall speak for himself. Alluding to certain words of St. Buonaventure, repeating the doctrine of St. Augustine as to the nature of the Light, and which are to the purpose that God is the Light which illumines, the Master who teaches, and the Truth which guides us, he says (vol. ii. p. 237):

"And here, in the first place, we cannot refrain from admiring the moderation of the Ontologists, who content themselves with inferring from these words that Ontologism is the doctrine of St. Buonaventure and St. Augustine, when they might infer that it is a doctrine which is *of Faith;* because the very same words are expressly found in the Holy Scriptures: ' I am the Way, the Truth, and the Life;' ' One is your Master, Who is in heaven;' ' He was the true Light,

Which enlighteneth every man,' &c. Hence, if the words given to God, of Light, Master, Truth, are *ipso-facto* proofs of Ontologism, Ontologism is a revealed Truth, and there is a new article to join on to the creed !"

Yes, the doctrine of Divine Concurrence is an article of Faith; but it is also a natural truth, and an article in the creed of civilised humanity. What purpose can it serve to throw this kind of dust in the reader's eyes? What is the relevancy of this talk about the Creed and the Faith *àpropos* of the opinions of St. Augustine and St. Buonaventure on the nature of the *Intellectus Agens* and the *Intellectus Possibilis*? The passage, taken apart from the context, might lead the reader to suppose that the question was about the supernatural enlightenment of Divine Grace. But F. Liberatore knows well enough it is about nothing of the kind. There is a natural Light, wherewith God "enlighteneth every man that cometh into this world." And what of it? What is its nature? Is it merely a power of the mind, or is it objective, and independent of the mind? This is the problem which we have chiefly to deal with; and it is the problem, not only of the present controversy, but of all philosophy. But we write not so much to solve it, as to state it (though we have our own opinion as to the solution); in order that such as may take part in the discussion may speak to the same purpose.

The term, "Lumen intellectûs" (we follow F. Liberatore), may be understood in two senses. It is either only another name for the intellectual faculty itself, or it signifies the medium of cognition. We have here to deal, it is plain, with the latter sense of the word. Now, what is to the human understanding the medium of cognition? First principles, perhaps : but these first principles, like every thing else, require a light in which they are manifested. "Omne quod manifestatur," says St. Thomas, "sub lumine quodam manifestatur."* And what, then, is this Light? F. Liberatore tells us that, according to St. Thomas, the Light is "a quality or permanent form" of the understanding. Although it proceeds from God, yet it is, in itself, a mere created thing. It is, in fact, nothing else than the Active

* Quoted by F. Liberatore from St. Thomas, Quæst *De Prophetiâ.*

Intellect (*intellectus agens*)—" Lux in quâ contemplamur veritatem est intellectus agens:"* which, readers of St. Thomas
know, is equivalent to saying that the Light is nothing else
than the power of abstraction. For it is the office of the
Active Intellect to abstract from the phantasms "intelligible
species" (or ideas), with which it informs the " Possible Intellect" (intellectus possibilis), thus making it intelligent *in act.*
Hear F. Liberatore :

" And thus, whenever he (St. Thomas) touches upon this
matter, he inculcates the same thing ; demonstrating promis-
cuously the existence of the Active Intellect and the Light of
Reason from the necessity of universalising the sensibles, in
order to render them objects of our intellect : nor does he make
this universalisation to consist in any thing else than in the
action abstractive of the *quiddity* from the elements which
singularise it in the concrete individuals."† And again : " To
illuminate, in things spiritual, is to manifest the object; but
the Active Intellect manifests the object to the Possible Intellect by the *abstraction* exercised upon the phantasms : therefore
this abstraction *is a true illumination.*"

The Ontologists must own the importance of this statement
of the case, which F. Liberatore supports by many and divers
quotations from St. Thomas, that the Light is nothing else
than the power of abstraction. If this be true, the " Angelic
Doctor" is far removed, indeed, from Ontologism. And why
should we doubt if it be true? The author does not blunder
about and misquote St. Thomas, as he blunders about and mis-
quotes St. Buonaventure. The matter of this second volume is
exceedingly good—at least, in general ; for we have already
exhibited one specimen to the contrary. We know quite
enough of St. Thomas to know that, as a rule, when F.
Liberatore differs from his opponents about what that writer
simply teaches, he is right and they are wrong. Whatever be
his weak points (and he has not a few), this, at any rate, is
his strong point—that he has St. Thomas, as the saying is,

* Quoted by F. Liberatore from St. Thomas, Quæst. *De Spirituali
Creaturâ.*

† *Conoscenza Intellettuale,* vol. ii. p. 294.

" at his fingers' ends." He is the formidable man of one book whom the proverb warns us against. But does not " a man of one book" mean a man of one idea? This, then, is the danger : a man of one idea will be sure to find his idea in the book, especially when the book carries with it the enormous authority of St. Thomas. Now, F. Liberatore's ruling idea seems to be this, that Deity must be strictly severed from immediate contact with the human intellect—else we are in Pantheism : while the aim of the Fathers seems to have been to establish the closest possible contact between Deity and the intellect. However, if we interpret SS. Augustine, Anselm, and Buonaventure by St. Thomas, and St. Thomas again by F. Liberatore, there is no closer union between God and the mind than this, that God has created man with the twofold faculty of perceiving sensible objects, and of arriving, by an abstractive process exercised upon these, at the higher intellectual notions. This doctrine stands on the same philosophical level as that of Mr. Mill; only Mr. Mill attributes the higher intellectual notions to association, instead of to abstraction. Now, let us suppose it true ; but what (once more) are we to think of the platonic language of the Fathers? Was this, after all, only what they meant in saying that the human mind is "immediately informed by," "conjoined to," and "lighted up" by "*the Incommutable Truth*,"—*that God has given to it the power of abstraction !* Why, if this be all, the same language might be applied to any system, short of Atheism. But would it not sound strange, to say the very least, supposing that (say) Condillac had asserted that the human mind is immediately conjoined with the Divine Mind, because God had created it with the faculty of *sensation?* Or, supposing Mr. Mill were to say that the rational soul was illumined "by the very Substance of God"—meaning that God had created it with the faculty of association? If this kind of interpretation be the only means of reconciling St. Thomas with St. Augustine (and F. Liberatore thinks they are perfectly reconcilable), we think it were far better to give up the attempt altogether. For our own part, we see little to object against M. Hauréau's view, that the system of St. Thomas is something "*mitoyen, éclectique*," between St. Augustine and the realists, and Aristotle and the conceptualists.

If, however, we must reconcile St. Augustine and St. Thomas, it can only be by supposing that when they speak of " the light," they are not really speaking of the same thing. For are there not *two lights*? The Fathers speak of the lamp of our mind as being enlightened by Another—by the Uncreated Light. Now, when St. Augustine or St. Anselm tells us that the Light is God Himself, they are speaking, surely, of the Uncreated Light, which is, as it were, the Sun of our intellect; and when, on the other hand, St. Thomas declares that the Light is the Active Intellect, that it is not one to all, but multiplied according to the number of individuals, he is speaking of the created light, which is a participation of God's Light. F. Liberatore himself helps us to this distinction by a reference to the article of St. Thomas about the " separated intellect." St. Thomas denies that the *intellectus agens* is one to all men; but he adds, " Oportet tamen quod ab uno principio derivetur." And what this principle is, he tells us in the most unmistakable terms : " Et sic illa communicatio hominum in primis intelligibilibus demonstrat unitatem intellectus separati QUEM PLATO COMPARAT SOLI, non autem unitatem intellectus agentis QUEM ARISTOTELES COMPARAT LUMINI." This is a most important passage ; it aims at nothing less than a reconciliation, by mediation, between Plato and Aristotle, and is an additional testimony to the eclectic temper of St. Thomas. Plato rightly said that God is the Sun of our intellect, which is common to all men ; and Aristotle also rightly said that its light is individually reflected by individual minds.

And the same distinction is also set forth in a most important passage of St. Buonaventure, to the consideration of whose teaching, as being thoroughly consonant (*in tutto e per tutto*) with St. Thomas, F. Liberatore returns in the second volume of his work. The Saint is discussing the nature of the Active Intellect. He first condemns the opinion of the Arabian commentators of Aristotle : " Quidam namque dicere voluerunt, quod Intellectus Agens sit Intelligentia Sepa-

rata, Intellectus autem Possibilis sit anima corpori conjuncta.
. . . . Sed iste dicendi modus falsus est et erroneus, sicut
supra probatum fuit (*Dist.* x.). Nulla enim substantia creata
potentiam habet illuminandi et perficiendi animam, proprie
loquendo ; immo, *secundum mentem, immediate habet a Deo
illuminari, sicut in multis locis Augustinus ostendit.* Alius
modus intelligendi est quod Intellectus Agens esset Ipse
Deus, Intellectus vero Possibilis esset animus noster. . . . .
' Erat Lux vera quæ illuminat omnem hominem venientem
in hunc mundum.' Iste autem modus dicendi, etsi *verum
ponat, et fidei Catholicæ consonum,* nihil tamen est ad propositum ; quia cum animæ nostræ data sit potentia ad intelli-
gendum, sicut aliis creaturis data est potentia ad alios actus ;
sic Deus, quamvis sit Principalis Operans in operatione cujus-
libet creaturæ, dedit tamen cuilibet vitam activam, per quam
exiret in operationem propriam ; sic credendum est indubi-
tanter, quod humanæ animæ non tantummodo dederit Intellectum Possibilem, sed etiam Agentem."

Now, observe, that we have no dispute with F. Liberatore about the meaning of this passage ; it is too clear to
admit of dispute. That it is God " who immediately enlightens and perfects the human soul," St. Buonaventure
says, is the opinion of St. Augustine. Nay, it is " true"
and " consonant with the Catholic Faith" to say, if you will,
that the Active Intellect is God, in the sense that He is the
Chief Agent (*Principalis Operans*) in it, and provided one
does not deny that God " has given to each creature an
active force by which it may go forth to its own operation ;" in
which latter sense (which alone concerned the point at issue
with the Arabians ; for the former makes nothing to the purpose), the Active Intellect is " simply something of our own
soul." If F. Liberatore wrote always consistently with the
doctrine expressed in this passage, we should have no quarrel
with him ; but if this doctrine is true, it seems to be a very
one-sided account of the Light of Reason, which makes it
consist in the power of abstraction. He says, however, that
there is " not a shadow of Ontologism in it ; and that it does
not prove St. Buonaventure to be Ontologist ; indeed, it proves

the contrary. ' Istc modus dicendi, etsi verum ponat, et
fidei Catholicæ consonum, nihil tamen est ad propositum.' Do
you hear? (ho says); the argument is beside the question.
. . . . . Because, although it be true that God is the Princi-
pal Operator in the actions of every creature, yet this does
not remove the fact that He has communicated to those creatures the active virtue which is necessary for their operation."
But do the Ontologists, while asserting with St. Buonaventure
that God is the Chief Agent in the Active Intellect, deny the
proper activity of such Intellect? Is this really the question
at issue, or any part of the question at issue, between the
psychologists and Ontologists? So we return to the original
question, What is Ontologism? For we are quite sure that
very many persons call themselves Ontologists because they
think, rightly or wrongly, that a mere psychological account
of the Necessary element in human thought is virtually athe-
istic, without the remotest intention either of asserting a
direct, immediate knowledge of God, or of denying the
proper activity of the human intellect.

But if it be asked, How can we, while endorsing the passages which we have cited from the Doctors of the Church, save
ourselves from the extreme doctrines condemned in Rome? If
God is the Light of intellect, how is it false to say that man has
a direct, immediate knowledge of him? " Si vidit Lucem et
Veritatem Tuam," as St. Anselm puts it, " vidit Te;" and yet,
" Nunquam vidi Te, Domine Deus meus." We never, however, considered this objection as presenting any real difficulty. God, under the aspect of Necessary Truth, is indeed
the Rule and Measure by which we think; but He is not
therefore, under such aspect, a direct, immediate object of
knowledge; He is merely the Rule and Measure. Here it
is the metaphor of Light that misleads. Corporeal Light is
a real object of vision; but not so the Intellectual Light of
Necessary Truth, which cannot be thought by us directly, but
only reflexly, and as the measure of contingent things. It is
for this reason that the pretended vision of God, asserted by
the Ontologists, when it comes to be expressed in language,
results in a vision of nothing. It is, notwithstanding, true

that God is "ever acting on the springs of thought"—as it has been well expressed by a writer above alluded to—even though He be "from thought concealed."

God, in short, is manifested in the human intellect, we should say, much in the same manner as He is manifested in the instincts of animals : or, at any rate, His influence in the latter case seems to us a good illustration of His influence in the former. He stands in the stead of a Reason to them (as Scripture teaches) which have none of their own ; and yet, so far from seeing God, they do not even know Him. Both these influences, moreover, have been exaggerated. As there have been ultra-Ontologists who have held the doctrine of a vision of God on earth, and pantheistic Ontologists who have identified the human with the Divine Intellect, because the former is "perfected" (the word, remember, is St. Buonaventure's) by the latter, so there have been philosophers who, for a similar reason, have identified the animal with the Divine Intellect : "Deus est anima brutorum," the reader will remember, is the motto of one of Addison's papers in the *Spectator*. So long as there are thinkers in the world, there will be errors. But, for our part, we frankly own ourselves as belonging to the number of those who think that the best of all means of refuting error is by the emphatic enunciation of that truth whereof it is the perversion or corruption.

But to return to F. Liberatore. Although he rather summarily dismisses the subject of the relation of the *Separated Intellect* to the *Intellectus Agens*, as being irrelevant to the controversy with the Ontologists, yet, as we have just seen, he endorses the unmistakable language of St. Buonaventure on the subject. And whatever doubt we may have ourselves, as to whether St. Thomas speaks quite so definitely as St. Buonaventure, he has simply none. He takes the latter as exponent of the former. According to this account of the matter, then, the Divine Mind, though "separated" from the human mind, in the sense that the latter has its own proper intelligence and activity, is yet immediately conjoined with our mind as the source of its illumination ("*immediatè habet a Deo illuminari*"). But how? that is the question.

In the sense that God has created us with the power of abstraction? This explanation, we have said, reduces the language of the Doctors to a bathos. Into the question of the truth or falsehood of the doctrine we shall not enter. But it would be interesting to know if this be really the teaching of St. Thomas, as F. Liberatore says that it is. It is the office of the Active Intellect, St. Thomas teaches, to manifest the object, by the abstractive process exercised on the phantasms. True; but is this meant to be regarded in the light of an adequate definition, either of the Active Intellect or its office? St. Thomas teaches repeatedly that its office is to abstract; but does he not teach, in other passages, that it has another office, besides that of abstracting? Does it not *illumine* as well as abstract? How can abstraction merely—which we had thought was rather a negative than a positive faculty, by which we cover, do not attend to, one part of our knowledge, while we attend to another—how can abstraction, merely, manifest any thing whatsoever? But no; we are wrong. St. Thomas teaches, it is true, that the Active Intellect illumines; then, it illumines by abstracting: there are not two acts, but one. The illumination *is* the abstraction. " The illuminative action of this light," says F. Liberatore, " does not consist in any thing else than in the primitive abstraction by which the quiddities or essences of things are made manifest." But if so, object the Rosminians, why then does St. Thomas, in one place, directly distinguish between the abstraction and the illumination of the Active Intellect? " Dicendum quod phantasmata *et illuminantur ab intellectu agente,* et ITERUM ab eis, per virtutem intellectûs agentis, species intelligibiles *abstrahuntur.* Illuminantur quidem : quia sicut pars sensitiva ex conjunctione ad intellectum efficitur virtuosior ; ita phantasmata virtute intellectûs agentis redduntur habilia ut ab eis intentiones intelligibiles abstrahantur."* Of course, the Rosminians maintain, according to the well-known theory, that the phantasms are illumined by being brought into conjunction with the idea of Being in general. But, waiv-

* *Summa,* 1, Qu. lxxxv. a. 1 ad 4.

ing this controversy, what rather interests us is the question whether St. Thomas teaches that the Active Intellect enlightens as well as abstracts, or enlightens merely by abstracting. We are also curious to see what device F. Liberatore will find now, when confronted with a statement of his author which certainly seems flatly opposed to his own theory.

He says that, granted that the passage may appear somewhat ambiguous, yet are we to set up a doubtful text of this kind against the many express statements of St. Thomas, that the intellect enlightens by abstracting? We must, however, submit that, for the reason assigned above, these statements by no means make so clearly in his favour as he supposes. And, besides, since we remember, not merely one or another passage, but a whole *article* of St. Thomas, in which he attributes to the Active Intellect a Light of which God is the Author and Source, we are quite prepared to find him distinguishing between the enlightenment which proceeds from such a Source, and abstraction which is a mere faculty of the soul. However, to escape the difficulty, F. Liberatore has recourse to a distinction. There is a radical or potential abstraction in which " the sensitive part, from its conjunction with the intellect, receives additional virtue ;" and then, by means of such conjunction, the phantasms are elevated and adapted to receive the formal illustration or abstraction. There is, however, no such distinction in St. Thomas. He says, indeed, that the phantasms are illumined by being brought into conjunction with the Active Intellect ; but he does not say that this illumination is by abstraction, either potential or formal. There was, in fact, no room for distinction between abstraction in this sense or in that, for he was arguing against those who denied that we understand by abstraction in any sense ; who said, " *Nullo modo* intelligimus abstrahendo a phantasmatibus.*" They argued that the Active Intellect stood to the phantasms as light stands to colours ; but the light abstracts nothing from the colours which it enlightens ; so neither does the Active Intellect abstract any thing from the phantasms which it enlightens.

St. Thomas answers clearly enough, to our mind, that the Active Intellect *both* enlightens *and* abstracts : " Dicendum quod phantasmata et illuminantur ab intellectu agente, et iterum . . . abstrahuntur." But the mode in which F. Liberatore gets rid of the objectionable *et iterum* is certainly noteworthy. "The word *iterum* (*di bel nuovo*)," he says, " would have no sense if the *abstrahuntur*, which he (St. Thomas) subjoins, did not itself import a new and more formal illumination of the phantasms." Now, remembering that, with F. Liberatore, illumination and abstraction are identical, his argument is this : The words, " the phantasms are abstracted *again*," would have *no sense*, unless they had been abstracted *before*—*i. e.* by that radical or potential abstraction, which he gratuitously attributes to St. Thomas to escape the objection of the Rosminians ! But is it " no sense" to say that the phantasms are *both* enlightened and *also* abstracted by the Active Intellect ; that it first does one thing to them, and then does another thing instead of repeating the same thing ? Of what use is it to argue further about what St. Thomas means, when it is clear that F. Liberatore can make him mean any thing that happens to suit his own purpose ? If there had been any such meaning as F. Liberatore supposes in the words quoted, certainly Cajetan would have discovered it. But this illustrious commentator distinguishes in the most definite manner between the illumination and the abstraction, and places the latter after the former. " The Active Intellect," he says, " assists and neighbours them [the phantasms],—yea, is conjoined with them with the conjunction whereby light is conjoined with colour,—and thus the phantasms are objectively illumined ; and by this objective illumination they reach the highest grade of spirituality, and thus become and are suitable that the intelligible species may be abstracted from them."[*]

Before concluding the present part of the subject, we will add to the testimony of Cajetan, that of an authority of our own day, who, like F. Liberatore himself, also appears as the apologist of the schoolmen. F. Kleutgen interprets the

[*] Commentarium, *in loc. citat.*

teaching of the Angelic Doctor as to the relation of the Active Intellect to the phantasms as follows :

" What, then, is the teaching of St. Thomas on this particular point ? He proposes to himself the following difficulty : Attributing to the Active Intellect the illumination of the sensible representations, it stands in the same relation with these representations as the light with colours. But the light abstracts nothing from the colours, but rather exercises upon them a certain influence. To which he answers with a distinction which was already contained in the words quoted" (*i. e.* the words of the passage in question). " The Active Intellect (thus he reasons), in turning towards the phantasms, by its inherent virtue produces the intelligible image in the Possible Intellect. Now, this turning of itself to the phantasms, and the consequent production of the intelligible image, come afterwards to be more definitely explained. The conversion is *the illumination which precedes the abstraction, rendering it possible;* the production of the intelligible image is the abstraction itself. Just as in Man the sensitive being becomes ennobled by union with the spiritual being, so also the sensible representations receive from the spiritual being such an aptitude as enables the intelligible image to be abstracted from them. Let us explain this thought by the similitude of corporeal light. The figure and the colour are always in the body perceived ; but it is only then, when the rays of light are shed upon the body itself, that our eye perceives the former and the latter. Blended with the light, they are manifest to sense. Thus, also, the object of the intellectual representation, that is to say, the quiddity or essence, is in the thing ; but in order that it become perceived by the intellect, it must be separated from those accidental properties with which it is concrete in the individual."[*]

It is clear, from this account, that F. Kleutgen considers that the illumination and abstraction are distinguished in the Thomistic Philosophy. It is only, we think, by recognising his distinction that we can possibly reconcile St. Thomas

[*] *La Filosofia Antica, Esposta e Difesa*, del P. Giuseppe Kleutgen, vol. i. p. 262.

with St. Augustine and St. Buonaventure ; and it is only, we also think, by recognising his distinction, that we can save this school of philosophy from being reduced to the godless psychologism which prevails in this country.

We have objected to the term " imitation" which our author sometimes assigns to the Light, as not being equivalent to the " participata similitudo" of St. Thomas, which latter certainly expresses a communion of some kind or other between the human and the Divine Mind. But, speaking merely of the human mind, and abstracting from such communion, there is no doubt that the " imitation" theory is that of St. Thomas. The dictum, *Quædam res imitatur quodam modo Deum*, may be taken as a summary of his teaching, and it is the basis of many of the instructive and beautiful analogies which abound in the writings of the schoolmen. But though the works of God resemble God, yet they are at best but a pale reflection of the glory of His Perfection : His attributes are simply incommunicable to creatures. The climax of perfection is to be, as the schoolmen taught that God is, Pure Act. In Him nothing is dormant, germinal, or potential ; every thing is *in act.* So that it is true to say of Him, not that He *has* His attributes, but rather that He *is* them. The Divine Intellect, then, is essentially in act. Next in order comes the Angelical Intellect, which, though it be not essentially in act, yet is always *actuated ;* while the lowest in order is the Human Intellect, which is, in itself, neither in act nor actuated, but a mere potentiality, capable of being actuated. As the Angelical imitates the Divine, and·the Human imitates the Angelical, so sensation imitates intellect ; and thus we are connected in the scale of things with our fellow-creatures the brutes, which have sensation, but not intellect. Intellect knows universals ; sense knows particulars. St. Thomas attributes knowledge to sensation, then ? Is not this what is called Sensationalism ?

Here is matter for a very pretty controversy between our author and his Ontologists. St. Thomas a sensationalist ! Well, F. Liberatore admits " that if to attribute knowledge to the senses be sensationalism, there is not a more downright sensationalist than St. Thomas," as may be shown from a multitude of passages from his writings. And what then? Did not all philosophers down to our own day assign, without any scruple, knowledge to sensation? But not only philosophers, the human race itself does the same. Do we not, for instance, does not the Holy Scripture, " attribute knowledge to the brutes, which certainly" (at least, so Aristotle taught, and the schoolmen after him) " are only endowed with sense?" " *The ox knoweth its owner, and the ass its master's crib.*" As to sensationalism—how is it sensationalism to allow an imperfect cognition to sense, provided we do not identify sense with intellect? " Is it wronging the sun to attribute a little splendour to the glow-worm?" Thus reasons our author. We suppose the Ontologists have adopted the modern, Kantian views of the relation of sense and intellect, in which the mere sensations, unenlightened by the intelligence, are said to be *blind*, and utterly incapable of thought, whether we use the word thought in the strict sense in which F. Liberatore uses it, as equivalent to judgment (for *pensare*, he says, is the frequentative form of the Latin *pendere*), or in the wider signification which attaches to the word, at least in our language. They would consider it to be equally false to attribute knowledge to sensation, as to attribute sensation to unorganised matter. As to the brutes, they must admit that these have knowledge, and therefore would ascribe to them a faculty somewhat higher than mere sensation, though lower than reason. But however this be, the Ontologists are evidently afraid of this doctrine of St. Thomas, which allows knowledge to sense, because they regard it in the light of letting in the thin end of the wedge, to use the popular phrase. They dread, if even the lowest degree of knowledge be attached to sense, that the reign may return of that degrading philosophy, the fundamental axiom of which was, *Penser c'est sentir.* In short, " If,"—says an Ontologist adversary whom F. Liberatore cites,—" if St. Thomas, in various passages of his works, has said that *the senses know*, it must be pardoned to the holy doctor, who was in a manner bound to the Aristotelian language ; but this is not to be tolerated in sound philosophers of our day, whose duty it is to preserve the propriety of language, in order to avoid the countenancing of errors already but too dominant." We had hoped that sensationalism, at least as a philosophy, instead of being dominant, was become obsolete. But, waiving this matter, we only wish to ask the disputants on either side a single question—and we ask it in all modesty, and as desirous of being set right if we are wrong : Is not the term " sensation" of the schoolmen equivalent to the term " perception" of our modern philosophers ? If this be the case (and, before reading this controversy, we had thought it was the case), the dispute is at an end.

But, to resume : the human intellect, being a mere potentiality, a mere *tabula rasa*, to use the Aristotelian phrase, there is desiderated a special faculty to render it into act. On the Platonic hypothesis of innate ideas, no such faculty would be requisite, because the intellect would be already in act, as informed by the ideas ; but the Aristotelian doctrine postulated the Active Intellect as a special faculty. Hence the distinction of the *Intellectus Possibilis* and the *Intellectus Agens*. When the senses, according to their office, have furnished the imagination with phantasms representative of the singulars perceived, the Active Intellect illumines them, and, by the abstractive process previously mentioned, rids them of their concrete, individual conditions. What it thus abstracts from the phantasms is the *quiddity* or essence of the thing—that which makes it to be what it is. In Socrates, for instance, it does not consider the particular aspect, features, character, proper to the individual. Sense considers these ; but intellect seizes on the type or model which is common to all men ; and thus the universal idea of *humanity* is, as it were, extracted from the singular. The Possible Intellect is passive as to the generation of knowledge, but not wholly passive ; it has an activity whereby it turns towards and desiderates the conjunction of the Active Intellect. In such conjunction, the latter informs it with the *universal*, and thus it passes out of potentiality into act ; and so knowledge is perfected. The Possible Intellect, it appears, is then the mere faculty of intelligence.

The schoolmen compared it to the eye, to which, as we have seen, the Active Intellect is as the light, and the objects as the colours.

This is the Aristotelian side in the eclecticism of St. Thomas ; but then, as F. Liberatore admits, he has also his Platonic side. He would no more have dreamed of contradicting St. Augustine than of contradicting Aristotle : it was his business so to explain the latter as to bring him into harmony with the former. Hence, with the qualifications above mentioned, the Platonic exemplars are retained. They are in the Divine Mind, as the sovereign archetypes and patterns of created things. As to the universal· *in re*, it is important to notice that this, in conformity with the " imitation" theory, is not identical with the Divine Idea itself, as the ultra-realists taught, but is a mere copy of the original in the Divine Mind. " Res naturales dicuntur esse veræ, secundum quod assequuntur *similitudinem* specierum quæ sunt in Mente Divinâ." Thus the True, the Good, and the Beautiful in created things are merely relative ; it is only in the " Principle of Cognition," in the Divine enlightenment of the Active Intellect, that the mind is admitted to a kind of participation (to speak doubtfully, as St. Thomas spoke) with the absolutely True, Good, and Beautiful. But, in created things, the mind only contemplates ideas which are at best imperfect copies. These are, however, perfectly reflected in the human intellect. The word " reflected" is here used advisedly ; for the mind resembles a mirror, in which the glass is as nothing, while the object reflected is every thing. This comparison of the mirror we do not remember to have seen in St. Thomas ; but it is, however, an excellent illustration of his teaching. It is reproduced from Balmez, and is the occasion of a controversy between our author and the Ontologists, both as to the teaching of St. Thomas, and the veracity of the doctrine itself. As to the teaching of St. Thomas, F. Liberatore is quite right : St. Thomas did not hold that ideas are, strictly speaking, the objects of our knowledge, but rather (he says so repeatedly) the media by which we know ; whereas the Ontologists maintained that they are the objects of our knowledge. Now, the ideas are as reflections in the mirror; but that which they reflect, that which we really know, is the object reflected, and nothing but the object. So far, then, our author is clearly in the right.

But now as to the doctrine itself; we hardly know if F. Liberatore rightly understands the drift of his opponents, and wherefore they accuse him (to use their own ugly word) of *subjectivism :* that is to say, they simply compare *him* with Kant, whose name he never mentions without abomination! Now, St. Thomas refuted Kant by anticipation. He denied the position, "quod vires cognoscitivæ in nobis nihil cognoscunt nisi propriam passionem." The mind no more knows itself merely in knowing the object, than the mirror reflects itself. What the mirror reflects (once more) is the object; and what the mind knows is the object—*quidditas rei materialis.* But the opponents would naturally insist: "Is the image reflected in the mirror really the object ? Is not the thing or person, whose image is reflected, the real object ? After all, what the mind really knows, according to your own showing, is not object, but image? And how do you know that it is really an image, a true copy of the original, since you do not know the original, but only the image ?" We do not propose to enter into the controversy. Whether the answer to this objection be easy or difficult, we do not find it in F. Liberatore. It is an objection of long standing against the common teaching of the schools, according to which knowledge, whether in the order of sense or in the order of intellect, is essentially representative. Matter, of itself, was held to be unknowable, unintelligible, according to the oft-repeated axiom, that the similar is only cognisable by the similar. What was, strictly speaking, intelligible was the phantasm *in actu secundo,* purified by conjunction with the Active Intellect : and what is the phantasm itself but *similitudo rei particularis ?* This is the constant teaching of St. Thomas ; while, according to the quaint notion favoured by St. Buonaventure, knowledge is the offspring of a marriage within the soul, in which the Active Intellect is Male, and the Possible Intellect Female.*

* " Est enim differentia in eis [ratione superiori et inferiori] secun-

But it is time to bring this portion of the subject to a close. For a more detailed—and, on the whole, for a very fair and interesting—account of the teaching of St. Thomas, we refer our readers to the work itself of F. Liberatore. But we would just ask one single question, before we part with the consideration of St. Thomas. Had he no faults? Did he avoid all error? Are we to follow him in every thing—even when, for instance, out of an excessive deference to the opinion of Aristotle, he teaches that it cannot be demonstrated by human reason that the world is not eternal ?*

The subject of this review would be incomplete without some general notice of the manner in which F. Liberatore treats the more modern opponents of his own teaching. Here, however, reappears his bad controversial side. We can cordially agree with most that he says on the subject of Malebranche; but we could wish that he were as large-minded as he is subtle-minded, and that he were as eager to see points of contact in doctrine as he is to see points of difference. Both Malebranche and F. Liberatore hold that representational theory of perception which philosophers of the present day consider to be exploded; and, this being the case, the controversy with Malebranche on the subject has

dum dispositiones et secundum officia. Secundum dispositiones, quia hæc fortis et illa debilis; secundum officia, quia hæc regit et illa regitur. Ratione diversæ dispositionis in debilitate et fortitudine, hæc vocatur Vir, et illa Mulier. Ratione diversitatis in officio et regimine, hæc vocatur superior, quia regit, et illa inferior, quia regitur. Talis autem dispositionum diversitas ortum habet, non ex diversitate naturæ, sed diversâ comparatione ejusdem potentiæ. Dum enim ratio nostra ad superiora convertitur, purgatur, et illuminatur, et perficitur. Dum leges æternas conspicit, et immutabilitatem divinæ virtutis et æquitatis, in bono fortificatur, et invigoratur. Dum autem ad hæc inferiora convertitur, utpote ad sensibilitatem et carnem quodam modo trahitur, et emollitur : et ideo sunt ejusdem naturæ ratio superior et inferior, differentes secundum fortitudinis et debilitatis dispositionem. Et quia una oritur ab alterâ, et ei conjungitur tamquam adjutorium simile sibi, rectè hæc dicitur Vir, et illa dicitur Mulier, et inter eas dicitur esse conjugium" (Comment. in lib. ii. *Sententiarum*, Dist. xxiv. Pars i. Qu. ii., *Resp. ad Argum.*).

* *Prim. Prim.* Qu. xlvi. Art. 2.

little interest for us. It does not matter much what kind of representational perception be held, when the question to be discussed is rather whether any kind should be held. Again, F. Liberatore attributes to Malebranche the doctrine that ideas are the proper objects of knowledge, instead of the means by which we know; yet it appears, even by the admission of our author himself, that Malebranche was not at issue with him on this point. He held that ideas are rather the means by which God manifests objects to the mind, than the objects themselves. It is true that, in one place, he calls ideas the objects of our knowledge; but the passage is easily explained. By idea, he says, he means " the object immediate, or nearest the spirit, when it perceives *some object*."* Now, it is the latter, the object perceived, which is the real object of knowledge. Then, as to the capital doctrine of the *Recherche de la Vérité*, Malebranche did not so much hold that the mind sees God, as that it sees all things *in God*. It is necessary to notice this, because there is a sense in which no Christian can deny the vision in God : it is simply the statement of that doctrine of Divine Concurrence which F. Liberatore himself reminds us is an article of faith. In God " we live and move and be ;" and this implies, that in Him also we think and reason. " Say not that you are your own light to yourself," says St. Augustine : " at most, you are but an eye. What avails an open, healthy eye, without the Light ?"† We may ask here, by the way, how this doctrine of St. Augustine accords with that of F. Liberatore, which makes the light to be something of our own, the mere faculty of abstraction ? It is not, therefore, in the statement of the doctrine of vision in God that Malebranche is wrong,—so far, he has Scripture

---

* *Recherche de la Vérité*, livre iii., seconde partie: *De l'Entendement pur*, chap. i. The following passage also expresses precisely the doctrine of F. Liberatore himself : " Outre qu'on peut dire, *qu'on ne voit pas tant les idées des choses, que les choses mêmes que les idées représentent :* car lorsqu'on voit un quarré, par exemple, on ne dit pas que l'on voit l'idée de ce quarré, qui est unie à l'esprit, mais seulement le quarré qui est au dehors."—*Ibid.*, livre iii.: *De l'Esprit pur*, part ii. chap. ii.

† *De Verbis Domini*, sermo lxvii. (*ordo vetus*), viii. (*ordo novus*).

and the Fathers on his side ; but when from the mere statement
of the doctrine he passes to the explanation of it, and abuses
that "Law of Parcimony," which has been called Occam's
razor, to the extent of admitting only one real cause in the
Universe,—a doctrine which is at the bottom of all his errors,
—then we are heartily with F. Liberatore. We also agree
with our author that Malebranche is, in his language at least,
decidedly Ontologistic. He claims for the mind, that is to
say, a direct, immediate knowledge of God as the Absolute
Truth ; but then we also feel convinced, as we have said before,
that, had some venerable Father or Doctor of the Church used
the language which Malebranche uses, F. Liberatore would
certainly have managed to let him go scot-free. For if,
as Malebranche says, we only know Necessary Truth "as
participable by created things," what, after all, does the
"direct, immediate knowledge of God," under the aspect of
Necessary Truth, amount to?

Though Malebranche is, according to our author, the
Father of Ontologism, yet he considers that its germ was
contained in the system of Descartes, for whose merits as a
philosopher F. Liberatore expresses the most decided contempt.
He either does not understand, or affects to misunderstand, the
nature of the Cartesian doubt, and is thus enabled to find con-
tradictions in the writings of this author to which both Cousin
and Balmez were blind. But let us pass now to the system
of Gioberti, which is the last expression of Ontologism.

The reader, who may have anticipated what kind of treat-
ment Gioberti was likely to receive at the hands of F. Liberatore, will be agreeably disappointed on reading the heading
of the chapter devoted to the consideration of the relation of
Giobertinianism with Pantheism, which reads thus : "Germs
of Pantheism contained in the Intuition." Only *germs* of
Pantheism! and in Gioberti! But, alas! the expectation
of any thing like moderation in F. Liberatore is doomed to
be quickly disappointed. He actually apologises for the mild-
ness of the sentence! If he were writing, he tells us, to
refute, not Gioberti's Ontologism, but Gioberti himself, he
would have been "more candid in the title of this chapter ;"

he would have ascribed to him, " not a seed of Pantheism, but Pantheism itself." He says that, to any one who carefully studies the *Introduzione allo studio di Filosofia* of that writer, " the tinsel of words vanishes, and the really Pantheistic foundation is manifest. And to show that this was the intention of Gioberti, there is no need of conjectures or of arguments ;" for Gioberti himself let out the secret (in what manner will be considered presently) that he was a Pantheist. Meantime, let the reader bear in mind that Gioberti wrote the work in question to refute that very Pantheism which F. Liberatore attributes to him. He wrote *professedly* to refute Pantheism ; he speaks on every occasion with the greatest abhorrence of Pantheism ; and yet we must suppose he was all the time a Pantheist at heart, and his intention was to aid Pantheism ! His mode of aiding it was somewhat singular : " Pantheism," he writes, " annihilates in effect the conception of God, although in appearance it exaggerates, increases the extension and importance of it. Hence, the rigorous Pantheist is necessarily Atheist, as we see in the case of Benedict Spinoza."* And, again : " If one neglects or repudiates this" (the dogma of Creation), " Pantheism is inevitable ; and Pantheism leads to Scepticism, to Atheism, and to other monstrosities of the Heterodox philosophy" (that of the German philosophers subsequent to Kant).† In short, we have carefully read Gioberti's work, and we solemnly declare that we find no more symptom of Pantheism in it than in this one of F. Liberatore ; on the contrary, we find in it principles manifestly repugnant to Pantheism, as was to have been expected from the nature and scope of the undertaking. Let Ontologism be ever so evil a thing, yet can any misstatement possibly avail to aid the spread of truth ?

However, F. Liberatore has evidently made up his mind that Pantheist Gioberti shall be, if he can possibly make him one ; if he is not one in fact, yet he can be made one by interpretation and construction. But how can you make out, even by argument, that a man is a Pantheist who admits such a duality in the " intuition" as that of the Necessary and the

- * Tom. i. p. 131.   † Tom. ii. p. 235.

Contingent—who attributes liberty to God and man—who holds, with Reid, that we immediately perceive this contingent world, and that God created it out of nothing—and who makes it an essential of his teaching, that the mind has an intuition of such creation out of nothing in the very notion of the Contingent as compared with the Necessary? How? Why, in this way: Gioberti's ideal formula is Ens-Creat-Existentias; but F. Liberatore thinks he has proved that the last two elements are superfluous in the "intuition"—that Gioberti could not, consistently with what he asserts of the first element, admit them. Well, suppose that F. Liberatore is right, what follows? He only proves that Gioberti is inconsistent; not that he teaches Pantheism. Are there not those who maintain that F. Liberatore is also inconsistent, and that, on the imitation hypothesis, he ought to be a "subjectivist"? Then, again, Gioberti maintains that "created things are, *by themselves*, unintelligible—a statement which is another path opened to Pantheism." Granted, for mere argument's sake; and granted, also, that Gioberti has words and phrases which, to one unacquainted with the Platonic language and symbolism which he affects, may seem to savour of Pantheism. Granted, in the same manner, that F. Liberatore is always right, and Gioberti always wrong, whenever they are at issue—that the latter is really open to the consequences imputed to him, and that he ought (always, of course, by construction) to have taught Pantheism. We are not the apologist of Gioberti, or the Ontologists: we only speak in the interests of truth, fair play, justice, and moderation; so that we will admit any thing, saving that Gioberti did teach Pantheism in the *Introduction.* We believe that, at the time he wrote this work,—to say the least,—he would with all his might and strength have put away from him that Pantheism which F. Liberatore so unjustifiably and ungenerously ascribes, not merely to his writings, but to himself.

But now hear F. Liberatore, as to how Gioberti let out the secret that he was a Pantheist at heart when he wrote the *Introduzione:*

" And to show that this was the intention of Gioberti, there is no need of conjectures or arguments, if we consider what, letting out the secret, ho has openly declared in his letter of *Demophilus to Young Italy*, saying, amongst other things, these express words : ' *I hold that Pantheism is the only true and sure philosophy.*' "

Then, at the foot of the page, we find a note to the effect that the authenticity of this document is " beyond all doubt ;" that, besides the testimony of the Mazzinians, who published it, it bears intrinsic marks that Gioberti was the author ; and besides, though " repeatedly invited to deny it, he never dared to do so." What say we to this ? What we say is, that it is to the very highest degree improbable that Gioberti should, with a single stroke of his pen, have simply nullified the work by which he had established for himself a European reputation as a philosopher ; still, it is not therefore impossible. But, whether it be true or false that Gioberti was the author of the document in question, F. Liberatore is certainly to blame for having made a most important accusation in a most slovenly manner. What are the " intrinsic marks" that this letter was written by Gioberti ? What authority is there for saying that he was taxed with the authorship, and never denied it ? And what is the value of the witness of the Mazzinians ? The whole affair bears marks of being a mere idle story. It is just as if somebody were to say that there existed somewhere a posthumous paper of Bishop Berkeley, in which that writer admitted that, after all, tho " Sceptics and Atheists" were right ; or that tar-water was an abomination, and that the Fenians had published the document. But, even granting again that F. Liberatore is right, how, in the name of reason, does this prove that he was a Pantheist at heart, that this was his " intention" in writing the *Introduzione* ?

One word as to the religious aspect of the question, which, naturally enough, gives a zest to the present controversy. We wish upon this, as upon other matters, to be on the right side, to think as the Church thinks : but then comes the question as to which is the right side. How does the Church think ? The proper ecclesiastical authority has, it is true, condemned what certain persons have called Ontologism ; but the Ontologism it has condemned—what they called Ontologism—is the system, the fundamental doctrine of which ascribes to man a direct, immediate knowledge of God; and this doctrine was only held by an extreme party in the school. The rest still contend, as stoutly as ever, that the Faith is imperilled by psychologism; while the psychologists maintain, with equal earnestness, that it is rather imperilled by Ontologism. On the side of Ontologism we are urged, in the name of religion, to reject the pernicious doctrine that the Light of Reason is a mere faculty of the mind; while, on the side of Psychologism, we are told that we open the door to Pantheism, unless we accept this doctrine. This is at present the philosophical situation, as far as religion is concerned. And this being the case, we think it advisable to keep religion as much as possible out of the question, until it be quite clear on which of the two sides our religious interests really lie.

445

POSTSCRIPTUM.[*]

SINCE the above criticism was committed to writing, an *Essay on First Principles*, by the Rev. Canon Walker, has appeared, exhibiting a view of the teaching of the Angelic Doctor so widely different from the one advocated in these pages, that we cannot forbear remarking upon it.

Canon Walker is a sensationalist, and he finds sensationalism in St. Thomas. Whether he would object to the name, we cannot tell; but we know not by what other word we can so aptly designate the doctrine maintained by him, that the knowledge of First Principles is due to sensible experience. That the writer should have discovered sensationalism in St. Thomas, no one will be surprised who is sufficiently familiar with speculative controversies to know how plausible a case may be made out by a judicious selection and skilful arrangement of texts. Now, St. Thomas certainly endorses the statement of Aristotle, that " Cognitio principiorum provenit nobis ex sensu," which, Canon Walker says, "is his own thesis *in ipsissimis verbis;*" but, then, St. Thomas endorses it with a most important distinction, which we do not find in Canon Walker's essay. In order to gather the whole meaning of St. Thomas, the above-cited passage must be collated with another. While affirming, with Aristotle, "quòd principium nostræ cognitionis est a sensu," yet, in answering the objection that intellectual cognition transcends sensibles, he says, " *Non potest dici quod sensibilis cognitio est totalis et perfecta causa intellectualis cognitionis, sed magis quodammodo est materia causæ,* . . . . requiritur enim Lumen intellectus agentis per quod immutabiliter veritatem in rebus mutabilibus cognoscamus, et discernamus ipsas res a similitudinibus rerum" (Prim. Part. tom. ii. Qu. lxxiv. Art. 6). As

[*] *Essay on First Principles*, by the Very Rev. John Canon Walker. Longmans, London.

thus explained, St. Thomas teaches that sensation is not the formal, but only the material, cause of our knowledge ; and this is the view opposed to sensationalism. It was therefore well said by Pacius : " Cognitio omnis a sensu *exordium*, a mente *originem* primam habet." Nor does the objection avail, urged by Canon Walker, that St. Thomas attributes the origin (using the express word) of knowledge to sensation, because the passage just cited from him shows that he spoke of the material and not of the formal origin of knowledge. This distinction was reiterated in modern times by Kant ; it was accepted by Rosmini and Balmez ; it was most emphatically insisted upon by the late Professor Ferrier, who arrogated to himself the merit of its discovery ; in short, it is the common teaching as to the general relation of sense and intellect. Surely Canon Walker must have been aware of the distinction ; yet he does not even mention it.* It is, notwithstanding, the answer to a good half of his pamphlet ; while much of the remainder, as occupying common ground with F. Liberatore, has been already considered by us. And the same distinction enables us to ascertain how St. Thomas could hold that the Active Intellect was a " habitus principiorum per se nota," consistently with his endorsing the Aristotelian axiom, " Nihil est in intellectu quod non prius fuerit in sensu." Canon Walker does not appear to us to realise the fact that the philosophy of St. Thomas is an essay towards harmonising

---

* He makes, it is true, a distinction (p. 4) between material and formal knowledge, according to which the latter is not merely to know, but to know the precise nature of what we know, instancing our Saviour's words to St. Philip: " Have I been so long a time with you, and you have not known Me?" But this has nothing to do with the distinction of St. Thomas. Canon Walker distinguishes between knowledge and knowledge ; whereas the distinction of St. Thomas regards, not knowledge, but the *cause* of knowledge. The nearest approach that Canon Walker makes towards a recognition of the distinction of St. Thomas, is in his Introduction (p. x.), wherein he says that sense furnishes the "materials for the Principles" of Reason ; and we would fain trust that he implies here an *à-priori* element in knowledge ; but he seems to contradict it again in another part (p. 61), where he states that even the Light of Reason is " derived, by created effects, from the Divine Light."

St. Augustine with Aristotle. This philosophy has, therefore,
two sides. While Canon Walker, in spite of his formidable
array of texts, has chiefly insisted on one, it has been our
care in the foregoing pages to exhibit somewhat of the other.
Let the reader judge between us.

And now we have only a parting word to add on the
subject of this pamphlet of Canon Walker. He alludes to
his former controversy on the matter in question, and the
little share of attention that his writings received, because
the stream was against him. He considers now that a reac-
tion has set in; he even seems to hint that the ecclesiastical
authorities have decided in his favour! We can only say,
that if he would merit the attention which he desiderates, and
which we also desiderate for him, he must, candidly and fairly,
meet the difficulties and objections to the empirical and representational hypotheses which are commonly urged by writers
of the opposite school. He is too good a scholar not to know
what they are. He cannot, surely, be unaware that the
objections urged by Cousin, for instance, against representa-
tionalism, do not tell merely against one or another form of
the doctrine, but against any and every form of it; and that,
consequently, his apology (p. 48) does not meet the require-
ments of the case. Then, again, he admits, of course, an
" objective or metaphysical truth," which, he says, " is necessary and eternal;" but, then, he tells us in the same breath,
as it were, that there is no such truth to our minds, for " the
subjective truth in finite beings cannot have the same necessity or eternity;" and he quotes, with approbation, the saying of Sir W. Hamilton, that " all necessity is, in fact, to us
subjective" (pp. 63, 64). How, then, we are forced to ask, do
we know that there is any objective necessary truth? Because
there is a God? But the objective *necessity* of our reasoning is
supposed in the proof of His existence: thus we should only be
arguing in a circle. No doubt Canon Walker has some answer
to this very obvious objection, which is satisfactory to his own
mind; but what is it?